HTML & JavaScript Practice Questions

E Evincepub
Publishing

Evincepub Publishing

SMIG - 65, Parijat Extension, Bilaspur, Chhattisgarh 495001

First Published by Evincepub Publishing 2017
Copyright © Dheeraj Singh 2017
All Rights Reserved.
ISBN: 978-1-5457-1047-0

HTML & JavaScript Practice Questions

By

Dheeraj Singh

About the Book

The book is a complete set of HTML and JavaScript Programming Examples. The examples are well tested and based on the syllabus of Masters Degree of Computer Science Students.

About the Author

Dheeraj Singh, an enthusiastic student and teacher, loves computers and programming languages like HTML, JavaScript, C, C++ and Java. He is having the post graduation degree on Economics. Despite of getting a degree in Economics, he is always found surrounded by computers. He is currently running his own tutorials on Programming Languages online. He has written this book at an early age of 20. The main aim of Dheeraj to write this book is to clear the small and necessary doubts of students willing to start programming in HTML and JavaScript.

Content List

S.N.	Program Name
	HTML
1.	Write a program to implement marquee tag with its attributes.
2.	Write a program to display class time table using HTML.
3.	Write a program to implement form using html.
4.	Write a program to implement <img> with its attributes.
5.	Write a program to implement subscript and superscript using html.
6.	Write a program to implement frames.
7.	Write a program to implement svg with html.

8.	Write a program to implement inline css.
9.	Write a program to implement internal css.
10.	write a program to implement external css.
	JAVA SCRIPT
11.	Write a program to show alert (), prompt () and confirm ().
12.	Write a program to display factorial number using recursive function.
13.	Write a program to find cube of the given number using function.
14.	Write a program to convert Celsius to Fahrenheit using function.
15.	Write a JavaScript program that accept two integers and display the larger using if () and else if ().
16.	Write a program to find Armstrong number of 3 digits using for loop.
17.	Write a JavaScript program to construct the following pattern, using a nested for loop.

18.	Write a JavaScript program to compute the greatest common divisor (GCD) of two positive integers using while loop.
19.	Write a JavaScript function to convert a decimal number to binary, hexadecimal or octal number using switch ().
20.	Write a JavaScript program to find the most frequent item of an array.
21.	Write a JavaScript function to get the number of days in a month.
22.	Write a JavaScript function to add specified minutes to a Date object.
23.	Write a program to display function of keyboard.
24.	Write a program to display mouse event using which property.
25.	Write a program to display load and unload event.
26.	Write a program Receive real data from the user and store it in a cookie.

27.	Write a program to Retrieves values from cookie.
28.	Write a program to check form validation.
29.	Write a program to display digital clock.
30.	Write a program to implement any two string method.
31.	Write a program to check whether number is even or odd.

1. Write a program to implement marquee tag with it's attributes.

<HTML>

  <HEAD>

    <TITLE>Maquee Tag Example!!!</TITLE>

  </HEAD>

  <BODY> <font color="blue"><marquee width="100%" height="15%" behavior="slide" direction="right" scrolldelay=10 scrollamount=8 loop=20>

      <h1>An Example of Marquee Tag ---></h1>

    </marquee>

    <marquee behavior="scroll" direction="left">

      <h1><--- Moving in Left Direction </h1>

    </marquee> </font>

    <marquee behavior="alternate">

      <h1><----Alternate Brhavior---></h1>

    </marquee>

  </BODY> </HTML>

Coding Output

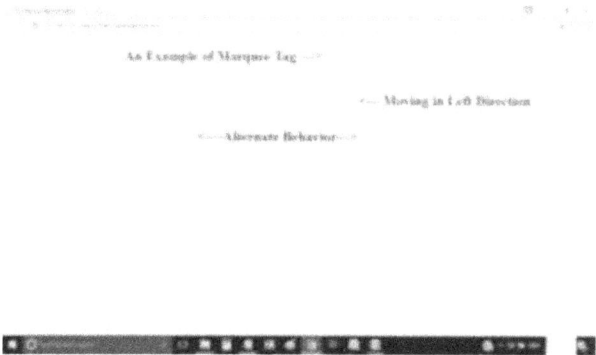

An Example of Marquee Tag ---->

<---- Moving in Left Direction

<----Alternate Behavior---->

2. Write a program to display class time table using HTML.

```
<HTML>
  <HEAD>
    <TITLE>CLASS TIME TABLE</TITLE>
  </HEAD>
  <BODY>
    <H2 align="center">MSc 2<SUP>nd</SUP>
SEMESTER </H2>
    <BR>
    <H4 align="center">Class Time Table</H4>
    <TABLE border=1 align="center">
      <tr>
        <th>DAY</th>
        <th>12:00-2:00</th>
        <th>2:00-2:45</th>
        <th>2:45-3:15</th>
        <th>3:15-4:30</th>
```

```html
    <th>4:30-5:00</th>

</tr>

<tr>

    <td>MONDAY</td>

    <td>OOPs LAB(batch I)</td>

    <td>TOC</td>

    <td>POS</td>

    <td>WT</td>

    <td>DM</td>

</tr>

<tr>

    <td>TUESDAY</td>

    <td>OOPs LAB(batch II)</td>

    <td>TOC</td>

    <td>OOP</td>

    <td>WT</td>

    <td>DM</td>

</tr>
```

```
<tr>

  <td>WEDNESDAY</td>

  <td>WT LAB(batch I)</td>

  <td>POS</td>

  <td>OOP</td>

  <td>WT</td>

  <td>DM</td>

</tr>

<tr>

  <td>THURSDAY</td>

  <td>-</td>

  <td>POS</td>

  <td>OOP</td>

  <td>TOC</td>

  <td>DM</td>

</tr>


<tr>
```

```
<td>FRIDAY</td>

<td>WT LAB(batch II)</td>

<td>POS</td>

<td>OOP</td>

<td>TOC</td>

<td>WT</td>

</tr>

</TABLE>

</BODY>

</HTML>
```

Coding Output

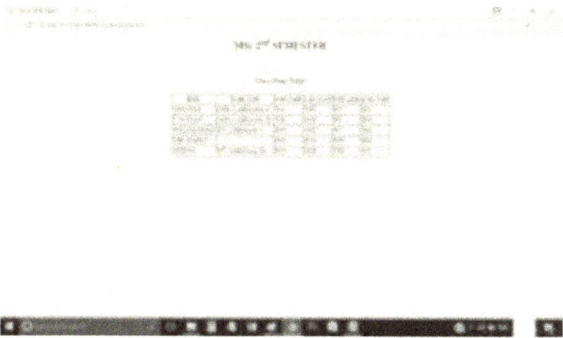

3. Write a program to implement a form using HTML.

```
<HTML>

  <HEAD>

    <TITLE>FORM EXAMPLE</TITLE>

  </HEAD>

  <BODY>

    <FORM>

      <H2 align="center">Employee Data</H2>

      <center>

        EMPLOYEE NAME :

        <input type="text" name="sname">

        <br><br>

        FATHER'S NAME :

        <input type="text" name="fname">

        <br><br>

        GENDER :
```

```
        <input type="radio" name="gendr"
value="male" checked>Male

        <input type="radio" name+"gendr"
value="femal">Female

        <br><br>

        Department :

        <select name=department>

            <option value="msc">SALES</option>

            <option
value="mca">ACCOUNT</option>

        </select>

        <br><br>

        HOBBY :

        <input type="checkbox" name="hoby"
value="singing" checked>Singing

        <input type="checkbox" name="hoby"
value="Dancing">Dancing

        <input type="checkbox" name="hoby"
value="Chess">Chess

        <br><br>
```

ADDRESS :

```
<textarea rows=3 name="add">

</textarea>

<br><br>
```

CREATE PASSWORD :

```
<input type="password" name="pwd">

<br><br>

<input type="reset" value="RESET">

<input type="submit" value="SUBMIT">

</center>

</FORM>

</BODY>

</HTML>
```

Coding Output

4. Write a program to implement img with it's attributes.

```
<HTML>

  <HEAD>

    <TITLE>IMG EXAMPLE</TITLE>

  </HEAD>

  <BODY>

    <center>

      <H2>image example</H2>

      <img src="sample.jpg" alt="sample"
width="200" height="200">

    </center>

  </BODY>

</HTML>
```

Coding Output

5. Write a program to implement subscript and superscript USING HTML.

```
<HTML>

  <HEAD>

    <TITLE>HTML Subscript and
superscript</TITLE>

  </HEAD>

  <BODY>

    <center>

      <H2>

        SUBSCRIPT : H<sub>2</sub>O =
H<sub>2</sub> + O

        <br><br>

        SUPERSCRIPT : 2<sup>4</sup> = 16

      </H2>

    </center>

  </BODY>

</HTML>
```

Coding Output

6. Write a program to implement frames in HTML.

```
<HTML>

  <HEAD>

    <TITLE>Frame Test...</TITLE></HEAD>

    <FRAMESET COLS="30%,70%">

      <FRAMESET ROWS="75%,25%">

        <FRAME SRC="1.html" NAME="menu">

        <FRAME SRC="2.html" NAME="logo">

      </FRAMESET>

      <FRAMESET ROWS="*">

        <FRAME SRC="3.html" NAME="main">

      </FRAMESET>

    </FRAMESET>

  </HEAD>

</HTML>
```

7. Write a program to implement SVG (Scalable Vector Graphics) in HTML.

```
<HTML>

  <HEAD>

    <TITLE>SVG EXAMPLE</TITLE>

  </HEAD>

  <BODY>

    <svg width="300" height="200">

      <polygon
points="100,10,40,180,190,60,10,60,160,180"
style="fill:lime;stroke:purple;stroke-width:5;fill-
rule:evenodd;" />

    </svg>

  </BODY>

</HTML>
```

Coding Output

8. Write a program to implement inline CSS in HTML.

```
<HTML>

  <HEAD>

    <TITLE>CSS EXAMPLE</TITLE>

  </HEAD>

  <BODY>

    <h1 style="background-color:#d0e4fe;font-
size:100px;"/>

      Inline CSS

    </h1>

  </BODY>

</HTML>
```

Coding Output

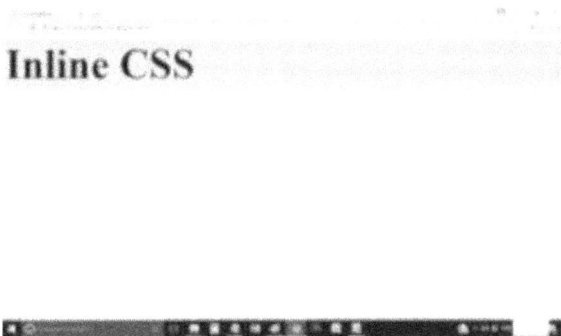

Inline CSS

9. Write a program to implement internal CSS in HTML.

```
<HTML>
  <HEAD>
    <TITLE>CSS EXAMPLE</TITLE>
    <style>
      h1
      {
        font-size: 100px;
        background-color: yellow;
      }
    </style>
  </HEAD>
  <BODY>
    <h1>
      Internal CSS
    </h1> </BODY>
  </HTML>
```

Coding Output

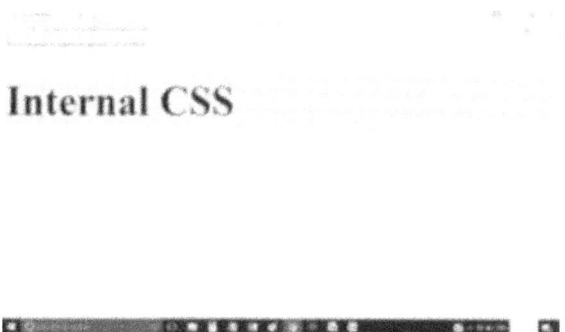

Internal CSS

10. Write a program to implement external CSS in HTML.

```
<HTML>

  <HEAD>

    <TITLE>CSS EXAMPLE</TITLE>

    <link href="extrnal.css" rel="stylesheet"
type="text/css">

  </HEAD>

  <BODY>

    <h1>

      External CSS

    </h1>

  </BODY>

</HTML>
```

extrnal.css

```
h1{ font-size: 200px;

   background-color: #d0e4fe;

   font-style:italic; }
```

Coding Output

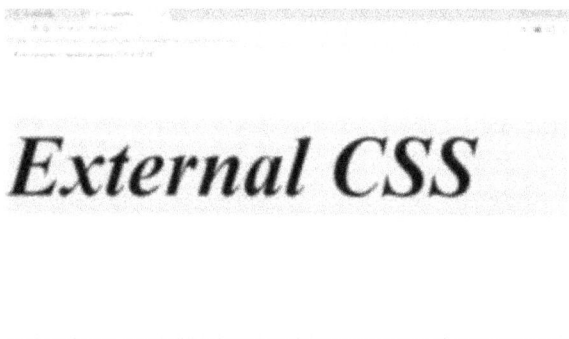

External CSS

11. Write a program to show alert(), prompt() and confirm().

```
<HTML>

  <HEAD>

    <TITLE>Predefined Functions</TITLE>

  </HEAD>

  <BODY>

    <script>

      alert("CONTINUE....?");

      var txt="";

      var name = prompt("Enter your name...");

      var b = confirm("Are you sure???");

      if(b) document.write("<h1>Welcome
"+name+"</h1>");

      else document.write("<h1>Input is
cacelled!!!!</h1>")

    </script>

  </BODY>
```

Coding Output

12. Write a program to factorial number using recursive function.

```
<HTML>
  <HEAD>
    <TITLE>Predefined Functions</TITLE>
    <script>
      function fun()
      {
        var n = document.getElementById("n").value;
        fact(n);
      }
      var f=1;
      function fact(n)
      {
        if(n>0)
        {
          f = f*n;
          fact(n-1);
```

```
            }

        else
document.getElementById("result").innerHTML =
"Factorial = "+f;

        }

    </script>

  </HEAD>

  <BODY>

    <br><br>

    Enter any number :

    <input type="text" id="n">

    <br><br>

    <input type="submit" value="Get Factorial"
Onclick="fun()">

    <h2 id="result"></h2>

  </BODY>

</HTML>
```

Coding Output

13. Write a program to find cube of the given number using function.

```
<HTML>

  <HEAD>

    <TITLE>Predefined Functions</TITLE>

    <script>

        function fun()

        {

            var n = document.getElementById("n").value;


document.getElementById("result").innerHTML =
"Result = "+n*n*n;

        }

    </script>

  </HEAD>

  <BODY>

    <br><br>

    Enter any number :

    <input type="text" id="n">
```

```
<br><br>

<input type="submit" value="Get_Cube"
Onclick="fun()">


<h2 id="result"></h2>

</BODY>

</HTML>
```

Coding Output

14. Write a program to convert Celsius to Fahrenheit using function.

```
<HTML>
  <HEAD>
    <TITLE>Predefined Functions</TITLE>
    <script>
      function fun()
      {
          var n = document.getElementById("n").value;

          var r = n*9/5 +32;

          document.getElementById("result").innerHTML
= "Result = "+r+" Fahrenheit";

      }
    </script>
  </HEAD>
  <BODY>
    <br><br>

    Enter any number :
```

```
<input type="text" id="n">

<br><br>

<input type="submit" value="Get_Cube"
Onclick="fun()">


<h2 id="result"></h2>
</BODY>
</HTML>
```

Coding Output

15. Write a program to input two integers and display the larger using if() and else if().

```
<HTML>
  <HEAD>
    <TITLE>Predefined Functions</TITLE>
  </HEAD>  <BODY>
    <script>
      var a = prompt("Enter first number....");

      var b = prompt("Enter second number....");

      if(a>b) document.write("<h2>"+a+" is greater than "+b+"</h2>");

      else if(b>a) document.write("<h2>"+b+" is greater than "+a+"</h2>");

      else document.write("<h2>both are equals</h2>");

    </script>
  </BODY>
</HTML>
```

Coding Output

16. Write a program to find out armstrong number of 3 digits using loop;

```
<HTML>

  <HEAD>

    <TITLE>Armstrong Numbers</TITLE>


  </HEAD>

  <BODY>

    <script>

      var i;

      document.write("<h2>Armstrong Numbers");


      for(i=1;i<=999;i++)

      {

        if(Math.floor(i/100) == Math.floor(i%10))

          {

            if(Math.floor(i/100)==0)
```

```
                document.write("<br>0"+i);

                else document.write("<br>"+i);

        }

    }


    </script>

  </BODY>

</HTML>
```

Coding Output

17. Write a javaScript program to construct the following pattern using nested for loop.

```
<HTML>

  <HEAD>

    <TITLE>Pattern</TITLE>

  </HEAD>

  <BODY>

    <script>

      var i,j;

      document.write("<h2>Pattern:<br>");

      for(i=0;i<10;i++)

      {

        for(j=0;j<=i;j++)

        document.write(" *");

        document.write("<br>");

      }

    </script>
```

```
</BODY>

</HTML>
```

Coding Output

18. Write a javascript program to compute the greatest common divisor(GCD) of two positive integers using while loop.

```
<HTML>

  <HEAD>

    <TITLE>Pattern</TITLE>

    <script>

      function gcd()

      {

        var x = document.getElementById("x").value;

        var y = document.getElementById("y").value;

        var hcf=1;

        if(x<y)

        {

          var t = x;

          x = y;

          y = t;
```

```
      }

      while(hcf!=0)

      {

         hcf = x%y;

         x = y;

         y = hcf;

      }

      document.getElementById("result").innerHTML
= "GCD = "+x;

      }

   </script>

  </HEAD>

  <BODY>

    <h2>

      Enter two numbers :

      <input type="text" id="x">

      <input type="text" id="y">

    </h2>
```

```
<br><br>

<input type="submit" value="Get GCD"
Onclick="gcd()">

<br><br>

<h2 id="result"></h2>
</BODY>

</HTML>
```

Coding Output

Enter two numbers :

30000

Enter two numbers :

300 40

GED = 1

19. Write a javascript function to convert a decimal number to binary, hexadecimal to octal number using switch case.

```
<HTML>

  <HEAD>

    <TITLE>Pattern</TITLE>

    <script>

      function convert()

      {

          var n = document.getElementById("x").value;

          var a = 0;

          if(document.getElementById("1").checked)

            a=1;

          else if(document.getElementById("2").checked)

            a=2;

          else if(document.getElementById("3").checked)
```

```
     a=3;
   switch(a)
   {
     case 1:
         var x=0,i=0;
         while(n>0)
         {
            x = x + n%2*Math.pow(10,i);
            n = Math.floor(n/2);
            i++;
         }
document.getElementById("result").innerHTML =
"Binary value : "+x;
            break;
         case 2:
            var x=0,i=0;
            while(n>0)
            {
```

```
            x = x + n%16*Math.pow(10,i);

            n = Math.floor(n/16);

            i++;

        }
```

```
document.getElementById("result").innerHTML =
"Hexadecimal value : "+x;
```

```
            break;

        case 3:

            var x=0,i=0;

            while(n>0)

            {

                x = x + n%8*Math.pow(10,i);

                n = Math.floor(n/8);

                i++;

            }
```

```
document.getElementById("result").innerHTML =
"Octal value : "+x;
```

```
            break;

        default:
document.getElementById("result").innerHTML =
"Please select converter type";

            }

        }

    </script>

  </HEAD>

  <BODY>

    <p>

      Enter two numbers :

      <input type="text" id="x">

      <br><br>

      <input type="radio" name="cnvrt" value="1"
id="1">Binary

      <input type="radio" name="cnvrt" value="2"
id="2">Hexadecimal

      <input type="radio" name="cnvrt" value="3"
id="3">Octal

    </p>
```

```
<br>

<input type="submit" value="Get GCD"
Onclick="convert()">

<br><br>

<h2 id="result"></h2>


</BODY>

</HTML>
```

Coding Output

20. Write a javascript program to find the most frequent item of an array.

```
<HTML>

  <HEAD>

    <TITLE>Array</TITLE>


  </HEAD>

  <BODY>

    <script>

      var arr = [3,2,3,2,2,2,2,2,4];

      var a=1,c=0,item=arr[0],i,j;


      for(i=0;i<arr.length;i++)

      {

         for(j=i;j<arr.length;j++)

         if(arr[i]==arr[j]) c++;

         if(c>a)

         {
```

```
        item = arr[i];

        a = c;

      }

      c=0;

   }

   alert("Most frequent item of array = "+item);

 </script>

</BODY>

</HTML>
```

Coding Output

21. Write a javascript function to get the number of days in month.

```
<HTML>

  <HEAD>

    <TITLE>Date</TITLE>

    <script>

      function getdays()

      {

        var m = document.getElementById("m").value;

        var y = document.getElementById("y").value;

        var day = new Date(y,m,0).getDate();

document.getElementById("result").innerHTML = day+" Days";

      }

    </script>

  </HEAD>

  <BODY>
```

```html
<p>

    Month :

    <input type="text" id="m">

    <br><br>

    Year :

    <input type="text" id="y">

    <br><br>

    <input type="submit" value="Get_Days"
Onclick="getdays()">

    <br>

    <h2 id="result"></h2>

  </p>

  </BODY>

</HTML>
```

Coding Output

22. Write a javascript function to add specified minutes to a Date object.

```
<HTML>

  <HEAD>

    <TITLE>Date</TITLE>

    <script>

      function add()

      {

        var m =
document.getElementById("m").value;

        var someDate = new Date();

someDate.setMinutes(someDate.getMinutes()+m);

document.getElementById("result").innerHTML =
"Minutes "+someDate.getMinutes();

      }

    </script>

  </HEAD>
```

```
<BODY>

  <p>

    Minutes to add :

    <input type="text" id="m">

    <br><br>

    <input type="submit" value="ADD"
Onclick="add()">

    <br>

    <h2 id="result"></h2>

  </p>

</BODY>

</HTML>
```

Coding Output

23. Write a program to display function of keyboard.

```
<html>

<head>

<script language="JavaScript">

function keyDown(){

alert("key pressed");

}

function keyUp(){

alert("key released");

}

function keypress(){

alert("key pressed and released");

}

</script>

</head>

<body>

<input type="text" OnkeyDown="keyDown()"><br>
```

```
<input type="text" OnkeyUp="keyUp()"><br>

<input type="text" Onkeypress="keypress()"><br>

</body>

</html>
```

Coding Output

24. Write a program to display mouse event using which property.

```
<html>

<head></head>

<body>

<div onmousedown="whichbutton(event)">click this
text with one of the mouse button to return number.

<p>1=the left mouse button</p>

<p>2=the middle mouse button</p>

<p>3=the right mouse button</p>

</div>

<p><strong>Note:</strong>The which property is not
supported by IE 8 or earlier versions</p>

<script language="JavaScript">

function whichbutton(event){

alert("you pressed button"+event.which);}

</script>

</body>

</html>
```

Coding Output

25. Write a program to display load and unload event.

```
<html>

<head>

<script language="JavaScript">

function load(){

alert("onload webpage");

}

function unload(){

alert("unload a webpage");

}

</script></head>

<body Onload="load()"
Onunload="unload()">

</body>

</html>
```

Coding Output

26. Write a program to receive real data from the user and store it in s cookie.

<html>

<head>

<title>JavaScript creating cookies - receive real data. example1</title>

</head>

<body>

<h1 style="color: red">JavaScript creating cookies, receive real data. - example1</h1>

<hr />

<script type="text/javascript">

//This is done to make the following JavaScript code compatible to XHTML. <![CDATA[

var visitor_name = prompt("What's your name?","");

var expr_date = new Date("July 30, 2017");

var cookie_date = expr_date.toUTCString();

final_cookie = "Name =" + encodeURIComponent(visitor_name) + ";expires_on = " + cookie_date;

```
document.cookie = final_cookie;

alert(final_cookie);

//]]>

</script>

</body>

</html>
```

Coding Output

27. Write a program to retrieve values from cookie.

```
<html>

<head>

<title>JavaScript : Retrieve values from a cookie -
example1</title>

</head>

<body>

<h1 style="color: red">JavaScript : Retrieve values from
a cookie - example1</h1>

<hr />

<script type="text/javascript">

//This is done to make the following JavaScript code
compatible to XHTML. <![CDATA[

var search_cookie = "my_cookie" + "="

if (document.cookie.length > 0)

{

// Search for a cookie.

offset = document.cookie.indexOf(search_cookie)
```

```
if (offset != -1)

{

offset += search_cookie.length

// set index of beginning of value

end = document.cookie.indexOf(";",offset)

if (end == -1)

{

end = document.cookie.length

}

alert(decodeURIComponent(document.cookie.substring(
offset, end)))

}

}

//]]>

</script>

</head>

</body>

</html>
```

Coding Output

Description : Retrieve values from a nested dictionary.

28. Write a javascript program to check form validation.

```
<HTML>

  <HEAD>

    <TITLE>FORM EXAMPLE</TITLE>

    <script>

      function validation()

      {

         var
x=document.forms["myForm"]["sname"].value;

         if(x==null||x=="")

            alert("Student Name must be fielled
Out!!!");

         x =
document.forms["myForm"]["fname"].value;

         alert("Father's Name must be fielled Out!!!");

         if(!document.getElementById("m").checked ||
!document.getElementById("f").checked)

            alert("Please select Gender");
```

```
        //Email Validation

x=document.forms["myForm"]["email"].value;

        var atpos=x.indexOf("@");

        var dotpos=x.lastIndexOf(".");

        if (atpos<1 || dotpos<atpos+2 ||
dotpos+2>=x.length)

        {

            alert("Not a valid e-mail address");

            return false;

        }

        var len
=document.forms["myForm"]["pwd"].length;

        if(len<8) alert("Your Password is week!!!");

        }

    </script>

  </HEAD>

  <BODY>

    <FORM name="myForm">
```

```
<H2 align="center">STUDENT
REGISTRATION</H2>

<center>

STUDENT NAME :

<input type="text" name="sname">

<br><br>

FATHER'S NAME :

<input type="text" name="fname">

<br><br>

GENDER :

<input type="radio" name="gendr"
value="male" checked id="m">Male

<input type="radio" name="gendr"
value="femal" id="f">Female

<br><br>

COURSE :

<select name=course>

    <option value="msc">MSC</option>

    <option value="mca">MCA</option>
```

\</select>

\
\

HOBBY :

\<input type="checkbox" name="hoby" value="singing" checked>Singing

\<input type="checkbox" name="hoby" value="Dancing">Dancing

\<input type="checkbox" name="hoby" value="Chess">Chess

\
\

Email Address :

\<input type="text" name="email">

\</textarea>

\
\

CREATE PASSWORD :

\<input type="password" name="pwd">

\
\

\<input type="reset" value="RESET">

\<input type="submit" value="SUBMIT" Onclick="validation()">

```
        </center>

    </FORM>

   </BODY>

</HTML>
```

Coding Output

29. Write a javascript program to display digital clock.

```
<HTML>

  <HEAD>

    <TITLE>Clock</TITLE>

    <script>

      function startTime()

      {

        var today=new Date();

        var h=today.getHours();

        var m=today.getMinutes();

        var s=today.getSeconds();

        // add a zero in front of numbers<10

        m=checkTime(m);

        s=checkTime(s);

document.getElementById('txt').innerHTML=h+":"+m+":"+s;

        t=setTimeout(function(){startTime()},500);
```

```
        }


        function checkTime(i)

        {

           if (i<10)

           {

              i="0" + i;

           }

        return i;

           }

      </script>

   </HEAD>

   <body onload="startTime()">


        <h1 align="center" id="txt"></div>

   </body>

</HTML>
```

Coding Output

30. Write a javascript program to implement any two string method.

```html
<HTML>

  <HEAD>

    <TITLE>Date</TITLE>

    <script>

      function strmethod()

      {

        var str =
document.getElementById("m").value;

        var txt = str.toUpperCase();

        var rpc = str.replace("kumar","Kaushik");

        document.getElementById("result").innerHTML
= "toUpperCase() : "+txt+"<br>replace() : "+rpc;

      }

    </script>

  </HEAD>

  <BODY>

    <p>
```

Enter String :

```
<input type="text" id="m">

<br><br>

<input type="submit" value="Apply_method"
Onclick="strmethod()">

<br>

<h2 id="result"></h2>

</p>

</BODY>

</HTML><HTML>

<HEAD>

<TITLE>Date</TITLE>

<script>

function strmethod()

{

var str =
document.getElementById("m").value;

var txt = str.toUpperCase();

var rpc = str.replace("kumar","Kaushik");
```

```
        document.getElementById("result").innerHTML
= "toUpperCase() : "+txt+"<br>replace() : "+rpc;

        }

    </script>

  </HEAD>

  <BODY>

    <p>

      Enter String :

      <input type="text" id="m">

      <br><br>

        <input type="submit" value="Apply_method"
Onclick="strmethod()">

      <br>

      <h2 id="result"></h2>

    </p>

  </BODY>

</HTML>
```

Coding Output

31. Write a javascript program to check whether the Number is even or odd.

```
<HTML>

  <HEAD>

    <TITLE>Even Odd</TITLE>

    <script>

      function check()

      {

        var n = document.getElementById("m").value;

        if(Math.floor(n%2)==0)

document.getElementById("result").innerHTML =
"Number is Even!!!";

        else
document.getElementById("result").innerHTML =
"Number is Odd!!!";

      }

    </script>

  </HEAD>

  <BODY>
```

```
<p>

    Enter any no.. :

    <input type="text" id="m">

    <br><br>

    <input type="submit" value="Even_or_Odd"
Onclick="check()">

    <br>

    <h2 id="result"></h2>

</p>

</BODY>

</HTML>
```

Coding Output

www.ingramcontent.com/pod-product-compliance
Lightning Source LLC
Chambersburg PA
CBHW020158200326
41521CB00006B/414